Rocks and Fossils

KINGFISHER

a Houghton Mifflin Company imprint
222 Berkeley Street
Boston, Massachusetts 02116
www.houghtonmifflinbooks.com

First published in hardcover as *Kingfisher Young Knowledge: Rocks and Fossils* in 2003
First published in this format in 2007
2 4 6 8 10 9 7 5 3 1

1TR/0107/PROSP/RNB(RNB)/140MA/F

LIBRARY OF CONGRESS CATALOGING-IN-PUBLICATION DATA
has been applied for.

ISBN 978-0-7534-6126-6

Senior editor: Carron Brown
Coordinating editor: Stephanie Pliakas
Designers: Melissa Alaverdy, Paul Akins
Picture manager: Cee Weston-Baker
Picture researcher: Rachael Swann
DTP manager: Nicky Studdart
DTP operator: Primrose Burton
Artwork archivists: Wendy Allison, Jenny Lord
Senior production controller: Nancy Roberts
Indexer: Chris Bernstein

Printed in China

Acknowledgments
The publishers would like to thank the following for permission to reproduce their material. Every care has been taken
to trace copyright holders. However, if there have been unintentional omissions or failure to trace copyright holders,
we apologize and will, if informed, endeavor to make corrections in any future edition.
b = bottom, *c* = center, *l* = left, *t* = top, *r* = right

pages: *cover* Corbis; 1 Corbis; 2–3 Corbis; 4–5 Geoscience Features; 6–7 Corbis; 7*br* C. & H. S. Pellant; 8–9 Corbis; 9*tr* G. Brad
Lewis/Science Photo Library; 10–11 (sky) Dynamic Graphic; 10*tr* C. & H. S. Pellant; 10*bl* Corbis; 11 Corbis; 12–13 Geoscience Features;
12*cl* C. & H. S. Pellant; 13*cl* C. & H. S. Pellant; 14–15 Corbis; 15*tl* C. & H. S. Pellant; 15*cr* Science Photo Library; 16*cl* C. & H. S. Pellant;
16–17 Corbis; 17*tl* Geoscience Features; 18–19 Corbis; 19*tl* Frank Lane Picture Library; 19*cr* Frank Lane Picture Library; 20–21 (sky) Dynamic
Graphic; 20–21 (rock) Science Photo Library; 21*tr* Corbis; 21*br* Corbis; 22–23 Corbis; 22*tl* Science Photo Library; 23*tr* Corbis; 24–25 Science
Photo Library; 25*tl* Digital Science; 25*br* Corbis; 26–27 Corbis; 26*bl* Corbis; 27*l* Corbis; 28–29 Corbis; 28*bl* David M. Dennis/Oxford Scientific
Films; 29*tl* Corbis; 30–31 Corbis; 30*b* Science Photo Library; 31*c* Corbis; 32–33 Corbis; 32*bl* Corbis; 33*b* Corbis; 34–35 Corbis; 34*br* Ardea;
35*tl* Science Photo Library; 35*r* Corbis; 36–37 Michael Fogden/Oxford Scientific Films; 37*t* Science Photo Library; 37*cr* Geoscience Features;
38–39 Corbis; 39*tr* Corbis; 39*cl* Science Photo Library; 40–41 David M. Dennis/Oxford Scientific Films; 40*b* Science Photo Library; 41*cr*
Science Photo Library; 42–43 Geoscience Features; 42*bl* Corbis; 43*tr* Corbis; 45*tr* Geoscience Features; 46*tr* Corbis; 48*l* Corbis.

Commissioned photography on pages 44–45 by Geoff Dann and on pages 46–47 by Andy Crawford.
Thank you to models Daniel Newton and Eleanor Davis.

SCIENCE KIDS

Rocks and Fossils

Chris Pellant

KINGFISHER
BOSTON

Contents

What is a rock?

Earth's crust is made of rocks. Some rocks are hard and solid such as granite. Others are soft such as sand. All rocks are made of minerals.

Rugged landscape

Here, in the Sierra Nevada mountains, weather has damaged a granite mountaintop and has broken it into large, rounded boulders.

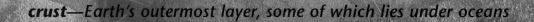

crust—Earth's outermost layer, some of which lies under oceans

Grains of granite

Granite is made of different colored minerals. The pink mineral is called feldspar, the gray one is called quartz, and the black one is called mica.

minerals—*natural substances on Earth's surface that form rocks*

Rocks from fire

When a volcano erupts,
red-hot lava bursts out and
gushes downhill as boiling
rivers of fire. Slowly the
lava cools and hardens
into rock. We call this
type of rock igneous,
which means "made
from fire."

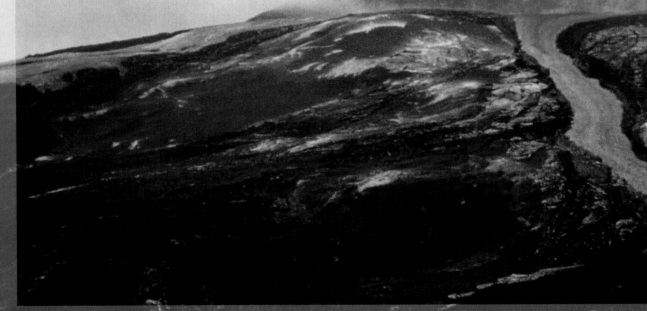

lava—molten rock on Earth's surface

Underground

Igneous rock also forms underground when molten (melted) rock, called magma, cools down.

Cooling lava

Lava takes a long time to cool. First a thick skin forms on top, and then slowly all of the lava turns into solid rock.

magma—molten rock when it is underground

Rough and smooth

As molten rock cools crystals are formed from the minerals. Large crystals grow if the rock cools slowly. Small crystals grow if the rock cools quickly.

Medium crystals
This microgranite rock has smaller crystals than granite because it has cooled more quickly.

Lava columns
Basalt has tiny crystals and can have a smooth surface. It often cools into six-sided columns.

crystals—hard, glasslike objects made of minerals

Cracks for climbing

Granite has large crystals. When granite magma cools, cracks form in the rock. Climbers grip the cracks as they climb.

columns—tall, narrow pillars

12 Secondhand rocks

Sand, mud, and pebbles in a river or lake or on the seabed can be turned into rocks called sedimentary rocks. These rocks can be told apart from others because they have layers, or strata.

Shell rock
Limestone is often made of tiny shells. Curved snail shells can be seen in this rock.

seabed—the bottom of the sea

sea cliff

Sandy cliffs
These cliffs in
Dorset, England,
are made of layers
of compressed sand
that formed on the
seabed millions
of years ago.

compressed—tightly pressed together

Layer by layer

There are three different types of sedimentary rocks. One type is made of the remains of dead sea animals. Another is made of mud, sand, or pebbles. The third is made when water evaporates.

Tiny creatures

Limestone is made of the skeletons of millions of tiny sea creatures. It is weathered easily, often forming scenery such as this picture below.

evaporates—when water turns to gas as it dries up

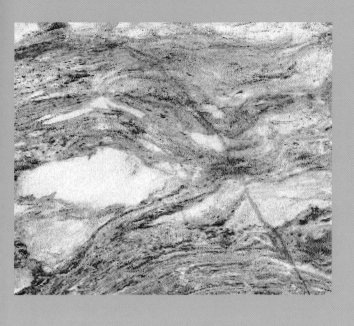

Rock gypsum

Seawater contains minerals. When it evaporates, minerals stay behind and form rocks such as gypsum.

Made of sand

Sandstone is a very common rock. It often forms colorful layers such as those you can see in this picture to the right.

weathered—to be damaged or broken down by the weather
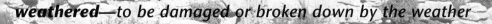

Rocks that change

Rocks change when they are heated deep underground—their crystals grow larger. Limestone, a sedimentary rock, turns into a metamorphic rock called marble. Layers in the rock disappear as it takes on a new form.

Fossil layers
Limestone is a rock formed in the sea that contains fossils. These fossils break down when the rock changes into marble.

fossil—any evidence of living things from the past

Smooth marble

Marble has millions of pale crystals made of a mineral called calcite stuck together tightly like a jigsaw puzzle.

Monumental rock

Marble is cut into many different shapes and is used to make ornaments, sculptures, and gravestones.

metamorphic—*a change of form, usually by heat or pressure*

Under pressure

As Earth's crust moves, any rocks deep underground are twisted and squashed, and their shape is changed by pressure.

Twisted gneiss

Gneiss rock has twisted bands of dark and pale minerals. It used to be granite and is formed by the greatest pressure.

pressure—when a weight is pressing down on something

Slivers of slate

Slate is made when the pressure underground is not very great. This rock breaks into thin slabs and can be used for roofing.

Silvery schist

Schist is formed in mountainous areas by medium pressure. Its silvery surface is covered with the mineral mica.

mountainous—*an area where there are mountains*

Wear and tear

Rocks do not last forever. They are battered by the sea on the coasts. High up in the mountains glaciers grind rocks into dust. Rivers carve valleys into the land.

Sandblasted

This arch is all that is left of a huge cliff. Sand carried in the wind blows against it constantly and wears it away.

glaciers—large, slow-moving masses of ice

Deep cuts

Rocks, sand, and pebbles carried in rivers pound against the riverbanks and can cut deep gorges into the land.

Wave power

Waves hurl rocks and stones at the cliffs, slowly breaking down the coastline.

gorges—*deep, steep-sided valleys carved into the land by a river*

Rain, roots, and ice

Growing roots
Plants grow in cracks in rocks. As their roots grow they push the cracks farther apart.

Rocks are damaged by the weather. They shrink in the cold and expand in the heat. Rainwater gets into cracks. When the water freezes, the ice expands the cracks, and the rock shatters.

expand—to get bigger

Icebreaker

This mountain ridge shows how ice can break rocks apart to form jagged points.

Washed away

This rock is a strange shape because rainwater has weathered it over many years.

Rocks from space

Space rocks come in many different shapes and sizes. They are called meteorites and are leftover rocks from when the planets formed. Sometimes meteorites crash down to Earth.

Big impact

This huge crater in Arizona was formed when a gigantic meteorite smashed into Earth. It is almost one mile wide—more than the length of 14 jumbo jets.

crater—a hole in the ground made by a meteorite or a volcanic explosion

Explosive rock

When large meteorites hit the ground, they explode. The heat from the explosion melts the rocks around them, creating glassy stones called tektites.

Hot metal

Most meteorites are made of metal, like this one. As they rush through the sky they become very hot and can be seen as trails of light.

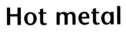

explode—to blow up, usually with a loud bang

The uses of rocks

Rocks are used in thousands of ways. Without rocks, there would be no bricks, cement, glass, or coal. Most industries are based on the use of rocks.

Crazy about clay
Clay is an important rock. As well as being used for pottery, it is used to make cement and even laundry detergent.

cement—a clay and limestone mixture that is used to make concrete

Angelic rock
Pale marble is a favorite rock used for carving into ornaments such as this angel.

Carved in stone
Many of the world's most beautiful buildings are made from cut rock. Sedimentary rocks can be cut into neat blocks for buildings, and all rocks can be carved into delicate shapes.

What is a fossil?

Any trace of a plant or animal that lived in the past is a fossil such as a shell preserved in rock layers for millions of years. The black impressions of delicate ferns and the enormous footprints of dinosaurs are also fossils.

Trilobite
This creature lived in the sea hundreds of millions of years ago. Its modern relatives include insects, crabs, and spiders.

preserved—*to be kept in good condition over a period of time*

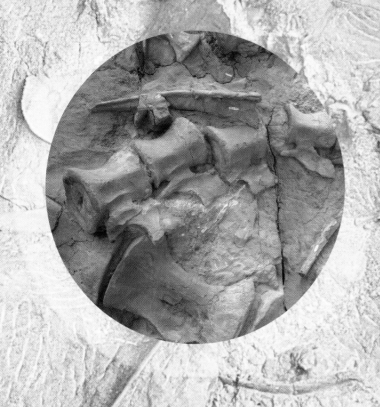

Big bones
These dinosaur bones were uncovered at the Dinosaur National Monument in Colorado.

Uncovering the past
A paleontologist works very carefully to expose part of a huge dinosaur skeleton at Dinosaur National Monument.

paleontologist—*someone who studies fossils*

How fossils form

Dead creatures and plants may be buried in sand or mud. This is when fossilization begins. The soft parts of the animal rot away, while the hard parts—its shell or bones— become fossilized.

Stuck fast and forever
This ant is caught in the sticky resin oozing from a tree. It will die there and may become a fossil.

Fossilized fly

Millions of years ago this
fly became trapped in resin,
which hardened to amber,
fossilizing the fly.

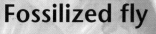

Ammonites

Ammonites swam in the sea when
dinosaurs roamed the land. They are
close relatives of squid and octopuses.

ammonite

resin—*a very sticky substance that oozes from pine trees*

Ancient sea creatures

Fossils of dead sea creatures lie buried under the constant buildup of muddy and sandy layers on the seabed. Trilobites, corals, mollusks, and starfish are all common fossils from the ancient seas.

Tropical fossils

Corals build their homes out of limestone, often in tropical seas. Fossil corals tell geologists where these seas were long ago.

mollusks—soft-bodied animals such as clams and slugs

fossilized fish

Stone starfish

Even delicate animals,
such as this starfish, can
be fossilized. This fossil
has formed in shale—a
sedimentary rock formed
on the seabed from
packed mud.

The age of dinosaurs

Nobody has ever
seen a dinosaur
because they became
extinct millions of years
ago. We only know
about dinosaurs
from finding fossils
of their bones,
footprints,
and eggs.

*dinosaur fossil
footprint*

Buried in rock

This *Stegosaurus* fossil
was found buried in
Wyoming. It clearly
shows the shape
of the dinosaur.

extinct—*when all animals or plants of a certain type die and none are left*

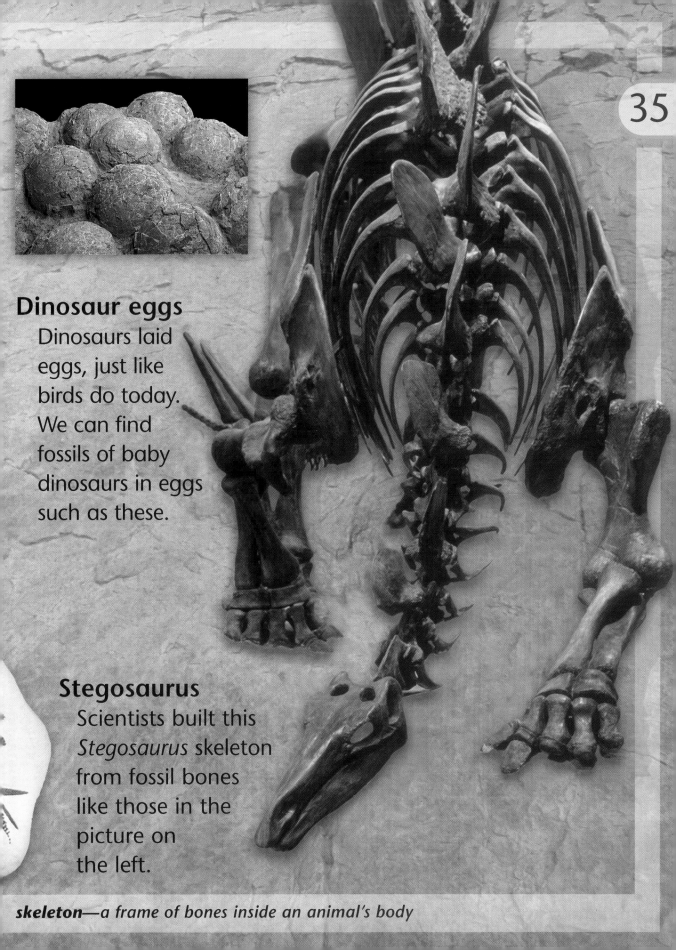

Dinosaur eggs

Dinosaurs laid eggs, just like birds do today. We can find fossils of baby dinosaurs in eggs such as these.

Stegosaurus

Scientists built this *Stegosaurus* skeleton from fossil bones like those in the picture on the left.

skeleton—*a frame of bones inside an animal's body*

Fossil plants

Fossils of stems and tree trunks are common, especially in rocks that contain seams of coal. Among the seams even fossils of delicate ferns may be found.

Stone trees

These trees were changed by fossilization—they are now made of a mineral called silica instead of wood.

seams—thin layers of a substance such as coal

From old . . .

Delicate, beautiful fern leaves are fossilized as thin layers of carbon between the layers of rock.

. . . to modern

A modern fern is just like fossil ferns that are hundreds of millions of years old.

carbon—a solid, black substance of which coal is made

Fossil **fuels**

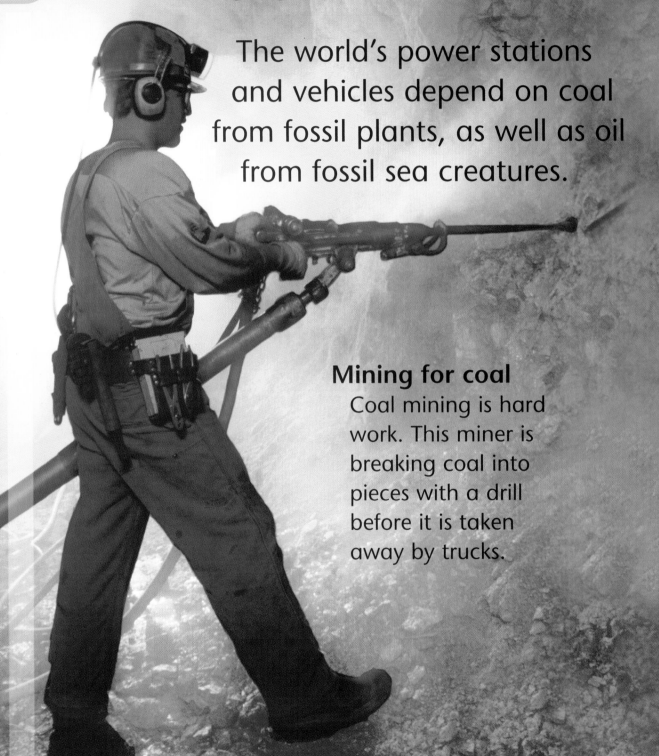

The world's power stations and vehicles depend on coal from fossil plants, as well as oil from fossil sea creatures.

Mining for coal
Coal mining is hard work. This miner is breaking coal into pieces with a drill before it is taken away by trucks.

fuels—substances used for producing heat or power by burning

Fossils for driving

Oil is a fossil fuel
from which many
products, including
gasoline, are made.

Poisonous fuel

Coal is a black shiny
rock. It has been
used as a fuel for
hundreds of years.
However, when it
burns, poisonous
smoke billows out
and causes a lot
of pollution.

pollution—*chemicals, gases, and other materials that damage the environment*

Clues from fossils

Fossils tell us about life millions of years ago. Scientists can reconstruct bodies of extinct creatures and study how animals and plants have evolved.

Alive and well

The coelacanth fish was known only as a fossil. Then, in 1938, living coelacanths were caught off the South African coast.

reconstruct—*to rebuild and show how something looked*

Historic footsteps

These footprints, made in soft mud over three million years ago, show that our ancestors walked upright at that time.

Archaeopteryx

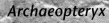

Archaeopteryx

This is one of the most famous fossils. The skeleton resembles a small dinosaur, but there are impressions of feathers. Experts believe that modern birds are descended from dinosaurs.

evolved—*to have changed gradually over time*

How to find fossils

Fossils can be found close to cliffs or quarries or in other areas that have sedimentary rocks. However, these can be dangerous places, and you must never visit them without an adult.

Cliff-hanger
Paleontologists go to many different places to search for fossils, and it can be dangerous work. This fossil hunter is carefully unearthing fossils on a steep slope.

quarries—places where stone is cut, usually for use in buildings

Beach treasure

Fossils may fall from cliffs and land below on the beaches. Be careful around cliffs, and beware of falling rocks.

Warning!

When rock is quarried, fossils are often unearthed. However, never go to working quarries—they can be very dangerous.

Fun with fossils

You will need
- 5 balls of modeling clay
- Shells

1

Roll the dough into flat cakes.
Sprinkle the first cake with shells.
These will be your fossils.

3

Push the sides together to make
an arch. This happens when rocks
are squeezed together.

Making mountains
Layers of rock can be squashed
together and forced up to make
mountains. Any fossils in the
layers then come to the surface.

2

Add two more layers of dough
and shells. Then put two layers
of dough on top. Do not put
any shells in the top two layers.

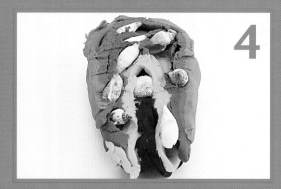

4

Ask an adult to slice off the top.
The first layers put down are now
in the middle. They are the oldest
layers and have the oldest fossils.

Amazing ammonites

Make your own fossil with modeling clay and plaster of paris. Use a real fossil or a shell to make a cast.

You will need

- Modeling clay
- Fossil or shell
- Plaster of paris
- Plastic cup and spoon
- Paint
- Paintbrush

Roll some modeling clay into a ball. Press your fossil or shell, patterned side down, into the clay to make the cast.

Mix some plaster of paris with water in a plastic cup and carefully spoon or pour it into the cast. Leave it to set.

Once your fossil has set hard carefully lift it up from the cast. You may be able to use the cast again to make more fossils.

Your fossil is now ready to paint. Use any colors you want. Copy the colors of the shell or fossil or paint it in brighter colors.

Rocks around you

Rock collection

When you start rock collecting, label your rocks and record where you found them in order to organize your collection.

An egg carton is an ideal place for your collection. Use a different carton for different types or colors of rocks. Paint your egg carton.

You will need
- Egg carton
- Paint
- Paintbrush
- Cup for holding water
- Magnifying glass
- Sticky labels
- Notebook
- Pen

Examine each rock using a magnifying glass. You may be able to see the different colored minerals that form the rock.

Number all of your rocks, starting from 1. Write the number of the rock on a sticky label and stick it onto the rock.